Dedicated to Leo Barnecut, for his wisdom, support, and courage

Please see YETItips.com for the latest in practical self-help and abuse recovery books.

ISBN-10:09840701-8-4

ISBN-13: 978-0-9840701-8-3

© 2014 Ann Ford. All rights reserved.

Big Hot Mess Borderlines

by Ann Ford M.S.

Contents

TRAITS OF BORDERLINE PERSONALITIES 7
THEIR QUEST FOR "EXCITEMENT" 9
DEFINING THE BORDERLINE BEHAVIORS 9
LOVE, AND CRUELTY 14
ADDICTED TO BAD BEHAVIORS 14
THEY CAN BE FUN AND DANGEROUS 16
BORDERLINES ARE VERY IMPULSIVE 18
MEDICATIONS AND ALTERNATIVES 19
EXCITEMENT CONFUSED WITH LOVE 21
BORDERLINES MAY CHEAT AT WORK 22
EXTRA TROUBLE IN MANY ENVIRONMENTS 23
LOVE IN COUPLES OR IN FAMILIES 29
MORE EXPLOITATION 33
WHEN FAMILIES GET HURT BY BORDERLINES 34
BORDERLINES CAN BE PUBLICLY HUMILIATING 35
WARNING TO CHILDREN OF BORDERLINES 36
BORDERLINES CAN EXHAUST KIDS 37
KIDS COPY BORDERLINE PARENTS 38
STRATEGIES AND TACTICS TO CONSIDER 39
BE WARY ABOUT GIFTS AND FAVORS 41
REMEMBER IT'S NOT YOUR FAULT 42
TIPS TO KEEP CALM 43
TIPS FOR YOUR PHYSICAL PROTECTION 44
TIPS TO PROTECT YOUR FEELINGS 45
BORDERLINES CAN CHANGE OVER TIME 46
BIBLIOGRAPHY 47
AUTHOR'S BIO 48

This book "BIG HOT MESS BORDERLINES" is about people with borderline personality disorder – the people who make others "walk on eggshells" around them.

If your life is being constantly disrupted by a person who enjoys chaos, and goofing off, and adores <u>drama</u> – particularly if it centers around them – but then can sometimes snap your head off with a mean remark – you might be being bothered by a borderline personality.

You may be experiencing an irritating neighbor, a boss that is constantly exaggerating your flaws and ignoring company rules, or you may know a date or mate who uses verbal put-downs or the threat of temper tantrums to try to control you – there are several classic ways borderlines try to control other people and there are millions of borderline personalities.

To check if the person is possibly a borderline, are you experiencing a person who:

- Sticks to You like Glue?
- Gets Angry Often?
- Does Verbal Put-downs?
- Does Bullying?

The problems would not be so serious except that the borderline personality disorder is a mental illness. The borderline personality person can be very destructive to others, and themselves, and two thirds of them are serious alcohol abusers – so they can run you down in their cars, with or without a road-rage incident.

Borderlines are characterized by having unregulated emotions, so they are sort of like the classic dramatist masks – happy in one mask, then tragic in the other mask.

The book refers to the "BIG HOT MESS BORDERLINES" because when the mental illness advances, the borderlines become habituated in their addictions – and 75% of them have serious substance addictions – they do more and more impulsive and destructive behavior to feel "high" and relieve their internal stress. When they get this advanced in their mental illness, you'll recognize them for being impulsive, manipulative, and for their delight in making other people feel smaller so they feel taller.

Why they are this way

Borderline disorder can be from (1) physiological and chemical shortages or (2) it can be caused by environmental factors – harm done to them. The disorder affects certain parts of the brain so that the person has impaired reasoning and emotional instability. They have poor relationships because their emotions are extreme and are not well controlled.

TRAITS OF BORDERLINE PERSONALITIES

The trait of alcoholism, and impulsiveness

Dr. Robert O. Friedel wrote: "...two thirds of (borderlines) seriously abused alcohol, street drugs, and prescribed drugs... Many people with borderline disorders say that such behaviors temporarily relieve the severe emotional pain they experience when under stress." Their high impulsivity makes them both self-destructive and other-destructive (from road-rage, to sabotaging people's careers, to telling lies to break up couples, etc.) and destroying property. Their impulsiveness is frequently fueled by drugs and predominantly alcohol. Alcohol is famous for providing (1) forgetfulness, and (2) brief feelings of intense pleasure. The borderline has a lot they want to forget. This is part of their attempt to *not* feel their conflicting and unregulated emotions, which leave them feeling highly distressed.

The trait of low level irritability – a form of chronic depression

This is a medically categorized "illness" that is treatable. Anti-depressant drugs are often prescribed and often work, but the borderline may stop taking them because the drugs remove the "manic" or wild-type-fun end of their emotional spectrum. The borderline may adore being manic, since it's high-energy and a more optimistic state than their usual state.

The trait that love runs hot and cold

The borderline's emotions are not regulated – they will love you one day and hate you the next day – making a person who is emotionally connected with them – very insecure. A borderline, when they become advanced in their mental illness, is not just a deeply flawed person, they can turn into being a "hater" and being constantly cruel.

The trait that borderlines fear abandonment, and have poor relationships

Suicide is a covert or overt threat from borderlines, and is tied into their deep and constant fear of being alone. Suicide threats may be used as a way of coercing people into staying with them and rescuing them, but they also do commit suicide, more than other types of mental illness personalities.

The trait that borderlines cause different types of co-dependent relationships

This is among their family members, children and spouses, and among their co-workers, bosses, and friends. The borderline does not want to be alone, and so they seek out co-dependents, and if they get the chance to "knee-cap" someone into making them a co-dependent, or at work if they put on a low ceiling or "glass ceiling" over an employee to keep the person around to serve their needs – then the borderline has relieved some of their abandonment anxiety – and caused flagrant co-dependence in other people's lives.

THEIR QUEST FOR "EXCITEMENT"

Borderlines make events unpredictable, because they bring the "chaos" with them. They have been described in two articles in Psychology Today in 2013, as being people who cause "chaos" around them.

The chaos referred to is their impulsiveness and the unpredictable things they will say – insults – or do – such as doing a strip-tease on a dare, in front of everyone.

The reality is that their behavior is planned chaos. Surprise is a unique type of control. The surprised person is at a disadvantage and can't defend themselves against the surprise actions or demands the borderline makes, which lets them get one over on another person.

They want to be the "stars" at any gathering, and want an audience and may have achieved powerful jobs, or "authority", as a result.

DEFINING THE BORDERLINE BEHAVIORS

According to the Diagnostic and Statistical Manual of Mental Disorders (DSM), which specifies diagnostic and statistical data for doctors, the borderline personality has a lack of concern about others, so it's easy for them to inflict mental hurt and physical harm. They also hurt themselves.

They get a "high" – and feel superior – it's a "high" of dopamine and adrenaline - when they do put-downs or hit someone.

An expert on borderline behavior, Dr. Robert O. Friedel, wrote that "...people with borderline personality disorder and veterans with Post Traumatic Stress Disorder, are either born with a fear system that is hyperactive, or it became hyperactive in response to early fear-provoking trauma, or both." This can be caused by a physically traumatic birth, or something biochemical that sets the amygdala in the brain into an excessively fearful response, and keeps emotions unregulated. A person who is a victim of repeated violence, is a likely borderline candidate.

Dr. Charles Whitfield studied over 30 years of research studies, and found that 80% of people with borderline disorder, were abused – as in sexually abused or physically beaten, as children.

There are possibly many ways that borderline personality disorder occurs – including a chemical shortage – as was mentioned – but in terms of psychologically driven behaviors, consider the following three possibilities.

ONE – Watch for bullying

The person has a fear system that is hyperactive in response to any trauma, that keeps the amygdala in the brain in a constantly over-aroused status, and leaves the person with wildly unregulated emotions, including intense rage or anger. This can apply to a person with PTSD (Post Traumatic Stress Disorder) as well as a person with borderline personality disorder.

Watch for degrees of bullying as a tip-off to how dangerous the borderline may be.

There are degrees of bullying. Sometimes a person will progress from the first stage of bullying – showing off to an "audience' to get a "dominance"' high, and go all the way to the ultimate form of dominance and kill someone – that's a psychopathic predator.

Bully #1	Bully #2	Bully #3 - Predator
Oblivious to what others feel – loves doing putdowns	Covertly mean – gossiping – some malice	Overtly cruel – malignant narcissist destruction

The first two categories of bullying can be confusing, because Bully #1 can be capable of receiving love from other people, and may be capable of giving some amounts of it. Bully #1 is limited by the degree of narcissism (self-centeredness) they live with.

Bully #2 is of the malignant narcissist category, which due to childhood deprivation or other cruel experiences, is solely intent on their own survival and their own feelings of being "powerful" or "dominant", and they are incapable of loving another person.

Bully #3 is a predator, and capable of severe destructiveness, and criminality.

TWO – Lack of compassion

The young man who committed the Newtown, CT murders, suffered from the biochemical disease of autism, possibly in the form of Aspergers. What is characteristic of autism, is that the part of the brain where human compassion develops – the insula region – is later in developing. Some autistic people develop it later as they mature, but they have to see examples of compassionate behavior, to even be able to copy it, and then do it. When a borderline consistently has no compassion for any living thing but his or herself, their mental illness is advanced.

THREE – Missing basic human drives

When bullying or cruelty is taken to extraordinary lows, as in criminal behavior, the borderline personality may have some additional psychological and physiological shortcomings.

They may be missing or have a very low amount, of one of the basic human drives: love and belonging. If they are lacking that, they can easily manipulate other people and think of them as mere objects for their convenience.

Emotional drives

There are many variations on the basic human emotions and human drives, but according to the in-depth research done by William Glasser, M.D., there are FOUR very deeply conditioned, and motivating drives. Some of these cause deep compassionate caring, and some of these cause deep cruelty.

Keeping in mind the research that has found borderlines to have been severely abused as children, 80% of the time, it is not surprising that some have been extraordinarily injured. A very damaged person can become so mentally ill that they find relief from their own pain by tormenting and terrifying others.

Generally, the more "playful" – and callously regarding other people as playthings – attitude combined with a HIGH drive to be competitive, and powerful, and have high personal freedom (be BEYOND society's rules) combines to fuel the drive of greatest cruelty.

LOVE, AND CRUELTY

POWER	FREEDOM
People who choose power can be violent, cruel, and can be MALIGNANT BORDERLINES	People who choose freedom can be callous
FUN AND COMPETITIVE	**LOVE AND BELONGING**
These people can be HIGHLY self-centered – they can often be MALIGNANT NARCISSISTS	These people often have more compassion for other people

The cruelest people have the lowest drive for LOVE AND BELONGING.

ADDICTED TO BAD BEHAVIORS

Alcoholism, substance abuse, and the Borderline person -

Dr. Robert O. Friedel wrote: "two thirds of (Borderlines) seriously abused alcohol, street drugs, and prescribed drugs… Many people with borderline disorders say that such behaviors temporarily relieve the severe emotional pain they experience when under stress." It's unfortunate that using drugs increases their impulsive behaviors, which causes borderlines a lot more emotional pain, disrupting their work and personal lives.

If you are involved with a borderline, this means that most of the time, the person is either "under the influence", or is just coming down from a high, or is impaired by the mental shortages that come with having a hangover. Alcohol makes a lot of "mean drunks", so you may be exposed to someone who is not only deeply flawed, but is, in fact a "hater" since they get so mean.

With someone that incapacitated, it is (1) okay not to "like" your loved ones, (2) it's okay to keep yourself safe by turning them in to human resources at work, or to a local hospital in private life, and (3) save yourself grief by limiting contact.

At work, you may have to find a new boss, and at home, you may have to keep away from a sibling who has not got their problems under control with medication and treatment, and you may have to be assertive and stand up for yourself with a senior relative and back away from their rage.

Remember that they will try almost anything – any substance – to feel better – looking for a feel-good thrill or "rush", making them dangerous to be around. They also usually have "cross-addictions" – multiple addictions – in their attempts to feel better – which can cause their physical health to deteriorate.

So for the majority of borderlines that you interact with, most of them are "under the influence" or are "coming down" from some substance abuse.

The chart of soft and hard addictions shows a lot of activities that many borderlines use to feel better. Lots of borderlines have drinking problems. What do you say about a recent DUI arrest, or what do you say when your relative is arrested or just released?

THEY CAN BE FUN AND DANGEROUS

Borderline personality disorder is common, and many people hold onto their jobs and families, even while they have this form of almost manic-depression. They're the life of the party sometimes, and they are raging anger-addicts at other times.

Sometimes this biochemical trait can be <u>helped a lot</u> by medication. Sometimes borderlines refuse medication, and they have to change jobs a lot, and get divorced a lot, and self-medicate a lot, with other activities and substances.

Most U.S. families are dysfunctional in some way, and the statistics are that 25% of the population periodically need medical mental health treatment, and another 25% of the citizens are sociopathic – they break a lot of social rules.

Famous for being super-impulsive, they take risks with their safety, everybody else's safety, and with money, and can seem to be super-happy when they take these risks.

If the family get-together is at a borderline's house, the party will be loud, there will be pranks, ass-grabbing, and lots of alcohol and smoking – or other substances.

The borderline dad is the one who tells the entire family gathering about his adult son's sexual rash – when he was sworn to secrecy.

These are some of the worlds most impulsive folks. If there's fresh snow on the street, the borderline parent will put the little kids on their skis, and tie a rope to the car, and drive around pulling them through the snow on the street. Nobody will be wearing a "helmet".

If they're athletic, they will compete at sports, or be competitive in other areas, to prove they are "special" or powerful. They may give their mates and kids great presents and money, in part to demonstrate how powerful they are.

Borderlines are very impulsive, because it makes them feel good. Having temper tantrums, and slapping, and doing put-downs – are all ways to feel "up" and happier, for the depressed borderline. They'll take risks, so they are the life of the party.

Research published by M.D. Charles Whitfield, found that 80% of borderlines were physically beaten as children, which reduces the ability to trust. Sometimes it can change with medication and therapy, or sometimes it's permanent.

The borderline personality usually had a very frightening childhood which may have caused, in addition to impulsiveness, a bit of ADD. Have sympathy for how bad they had it – but they're not entitled to hurt you.

BORDERLINES ARE VERY IMPULSIVE

The DSM mental health manual states that borderlines show:

"Impulsivity in at least 2 areas (e.g. spending, sex, reckless driving, substance abuse, binge eating)"

"Unstable relationships alternating with extremes of praise and devaluation" [they have a high divorce rate] and it can hinge on "their unstable self image or sense of self" and their desire for excessive amounts of attention

Like other narcissists, they are: "exploitive of others to get their own ends", with "unreasonable expectations".

"Have stress-related paranoia"; "don't trust other people"; can "lack empathy and be unwilling to identify with the feelings and needs of others." "Disregards others."

"Shows intense anger, can't control it, has physical fights."

MEDICATIONS AND ALTERNATIVES

For the 75% of borderlines who are self-medicating for their emotional pain with alcohol, there is a drug that has been very effective in correcting the problem. A famous French M.D., who also practices in the U.S., Dr. Olivier Ameisen, spent years after his glittering career as one of the world's leading heart surgeons, collapsed from drinking to excess. He found that the drug baclofen cured all his cravings, and restored the quality of his life.

Borderlines can take medication, and their doctors often urge them to, since "meds" bring down impulsiveness. But borderlines prefer not taking medication because their manic "highs" are much higher without medication.

It is not enough to try to understand what the borderlines need, because dealing with their mental health puts the average person way in over their head. It is important to get borderlines to professionals, and to take care of your own anxieties, caused by being around them.

OTHER ALTERNATIVES

There are other treatments that work on borderlines to reduce their anxiety and impulsiveness. Some of these are advised for those reducing anxiety for those of us who have to *around* borderlines.

A supplement that benefits the borderline, and the borderline's victim, is 5-HTP, which calms anxiety.

It is also a well-kept secret that acupuncture treatment can help cure abnormal mental states and can cure alcoholism.

EMDR has been used successfully on Post Traumatic Stress Victims, in less than a few weeks. By teaching a person to follow another person's moving finger, or by teaching a person to tap their knees alternately – you are interrupting a mental habit of emotionally welling up to a painful thought, or memory. You are changing the focus to another sensation, and lessening the impact of the anxious thought or memory – which is how the trauma is reduced.

Using the EFT – Emotional Freedom Technique (free on the Internet), one learns to tap the eyebrows and cheekbones and hands, in ways that ALSO distract from the anxious thought, at the same time that you say to yourself affirming statements such as "I'm an adult now, I have skills to handle this." Also, walking up a steep hill pulls blood to the lower body, and a person calms down.

You can somewhat control borderline behaviors by having every moment filled with a planned activity, and if there is a gap in the action, ask them to tell a story or tell a joke. They love being the center of attention.

Do NOT leave them alone – they'll act out.

EXCITEMENT CONFUSED WITH LOVE

Remember that most borderlines drink, which increases their depression, and depressed parents punish 4 times more than non-depressed parents.

They want stimulation to not feel depressed, so that 74% of the parents or older adults, who can afford it in retirement, choose to NOT live near their immediate families. They have exhausted their families. As one 70 year old brother said about his sister: "she's an awful person. I don't want to be around her ever."

They often don't take prescribed medications for their bad moods and extreme anger, so their behaviors can be corrosive and cruel.

Don't feel any false loyalty, just ignore what they say, their actions show that family members are not a "love" priority, but are convenient. They often don't love, but with people they have attachments, unless they change with therapy and medication.

Their family members usually need therapy to "get over" them.

BORDERLINES MAY CHEAT AT WORK

When one woman stole gems from the jewelry store she'd worked at for 30 years, she said she was "very sorry". YOU can say: "Something came over her, a type of illness, so she couldn't control herself." You don't owe more information.

When a woman embezzled from the coffee company she worked for, and ordered lots of expensive stuff, she said she "was sorry." As a relative, YOU can say: "She was a very generous and confused person – she gave a lot of what she got, to other people. She's paying her debt to society in jail right now. End of discussion."

There are some great athletes who are borderlines, and have ADHD, and they hurt and cheat others, from their competitors to their sponsors. Lance Armstrong is an example.

From the perspective of the mentally ill borderline, they are just doing what they assume anybody would do, if they were in their position.

Have you played tennis with a borderline and had your shots called out, when they were in? If so, that's the norm. They find "cheating" a very fun "high" of being superior to other people. As one said: "Everyone cheats at golf!" but only he did, and so got rejected.

EXTRA TROUBLE IN MANY ENVIRONMENTS

There are many folks with borderline personality disorder, and some are our relatives. You may be living with one (or more) at home. Although smart, they have big anger issues. One former CEO, after being fired, took out his anger on his teenage son and stabbed him in the stomach. Borderlines often wish they had the power of (1) attorneys or (2) M.D.s, but most work in business, trying to put one over on someone else.

One college age son found that his father was deducting all four of his children – though none of them lived at home – in fraudulent IRS deductions. The son had to decide to keep his dad's cheating secret or not.

Prisons host many borderlines, along with more scary psychopathic killers. Borderlines are often in white collar prisons for tax evasion. As one millionaire said: "I love an audit, where I can beat the IRS at their own game." They will try to "cheat" relatives too – for sport.

Borderlines will work very hard to get positions of power, and they love aggressive competition so you can run into them as bosses, quite regularly.

EXAMPLE OF A BORDERLINE BOSS:

Hank called in his contractor Roger, and read him the riot act for not being more communicative – which meant coming in every day at the end of the day and bowing and scraping and flattering Hank – and maybe being forced to have a drink with him, as he pulled a bottle and glasses off his bookshelf.

Roger was a contractor because he needed the money, but he was resisting being an employee because he thought this boss was a "sicko".

So Hank, after his normal drink at lunch, called Roger into a conference room one afternoon , and proceeded to give himself a little "power rush" by trying to make Roger feel smaller so he – Hank – could feel taller. He criticized Roger's work, all the while standing on a chair in the conference room and shouting!

# # #

EXAMPLE OF A BORDERLINE CONSULTANT:

Susan had been let go from her bank manager position with one bank, although her aggressive style had made her responsible for a lot of the bank's loans. But she was too aggressive. She never shared credit on any work projects, and she even swiped credit for other people's work. Eventually that was noticed, and so when the downsizing came, she was let go. Another bank quickly hired her, and she proceeded to do more of her "questionable" behaviors. She promised one client, Tim, he could have a bank office rent-free since he was running a not-for-profit, and their space was empty, and the bank could take the write-off. Then 5 months later, she got greedy to show that she was making some revenue for the bank, and changed her mind, lied that she had spoken to Tim about it, and socked him with a giant rent bill for several months rent. A bill big enough to kill a small business like his.

Bankers have a position of power that they can abuse if they wish to – and many of them do abuse it – if they are borderlines.

With someone so consistently dishonest – she lied a lot of the time – the chances of Tim getting out of the relationship with his money back, were highly unlikely. So he paid it, and just avoided her like the plague. She continued her career progression, every couple of years, changing her employer, which is characteristic of many borderlines. Just when people start to catch on to some questionable behaviors, many of them move to a new position.

She also put people down verbally all the time. She did particularly mean verbal put-downs when she talked about her house husband. What this illustrates is the constantly changing emotional states of the borderline – their emotions are unregulated – and they can go from liking you to hating you – in an instant.

# # #

EXAMPLE OF A BORDERLINE DRUNK BOSS:

Dick was a borderline who fell into the category of the 75% of borderlines who drink a lot of alcohol to self-medicate. He drank every lunch time, and every late afternoon, and every morning he was cranky and hung-over till noon.

He loved showing that he had symbols of power, and had huge photos blown up of his house and boat, on the walls of his office, in a building where people were not supposed to post photos on the walls.

He would routinely give reviews of his employees that were low and mean – because he was usually in a mean mood – and usually "under the influence". He would also "keep" very high producing employees by giving one critical comment on a review – "knee-capping" them – so that they could not move to another department. This way he kept competent people who he would exploit to rescue him, since he was able to do less and less of his job with any competence.

He adored showing off what power he had. He stood in the open hallway and shouted to anybody walking by: "I don't care what they say, I make my own rules!" as if he was a dictator or a king.

# # #

EXAMPLE OF A BORDERLINE BOSS SEX ADDICT:

Dave was a manager at an advertising agency, and a talented female in another department was interested in working for his department. He invited her to a business lunch. She accepted, thinking it was no big deal.

They went in his car, and he took her to a porn shop. They walked in past a display case of hundreds of sex toys, and there were all sorts of rooms and booths with people in them.

He paid for a room, and they went into room and watched a giant screen porno movie. He was smiling the whole time, and not talking. She said very little and just tried to keep nonchalant.

She had seen sex addicts before. She had had a boss once who borrowed another employee's car, and broke the front seat lever, when he shoved it back, when he drove to a red light district to get serviced in the car by a prostitute, on his lunch hour.

At the end of the movie they left and he drove them back to the advertising agency, and no mention of it was every made by either of them – she was discreet – and of course, she didn't want to work for him, after that.

Borderlines are usually cross-addicted – having multiple addictions – so if you observe one addiction, you can expect there to be at least one or two others that you have yet to discover.

# # #

YOUR NEXT BORDERLINE BOSS

When you have worked with a borderline, you have to make the decision of what you are going to do when you next encounter a borderline boss. One executive recruiter actually was candid with a job candidate and said: "Honestly, I could lose my job for saying this, but you should definitely turn this job down. You will grow to hate this man and he will make your work life a living hell."

The producer, Emmy Award winning television host, and comedic movie star Tina Fey, wrote in her book Bossypants about working with brutal people: "I admit that as a producer I have a tacit "no hot-heads" policy. For years, to be considered to be a genius at comedy people had to be dangerous and unpredictable." She mentioned getting screamed at and how she didn't want to experience it again. "I have met some very dangerous, erratic, funny people over the years, people I admire, but I don't want to work with them every day."

LOVE IN COUPLES OR IN FAMILIES

It's Okay to not "like" your loved ones.

Family get-togethers bring up a lot of familiar "myths" about how close the family is, or how funny some disastrous action was, that was actually mean. A person who's mean on purpose, may be a borderline.

Have you sat down at a family get-together – even playing a Christmas board game – and found that one person was blatantly cheating? That's the borderline, who thinks that no one knows – so they give themselves a little superiority boost.

Another way that borderlines cheat, is on their lovers and spouses. Arnold Schwarzenegger cheated with his housekeeper, and others. One of his sons changed his last name out of shame. Impulsivity is VERY high with borderlines so they have a lot of break-ups. Being impulsive is a big determinant of sexual and emotional "cheating".

Watch for the laughing father who is putting down his teenage son, saying: "You're no rocket boy!" That's mean.

Or when you hear the rich mother-in-law, trash-talking her daughter-in-law: "…she's from peasant stock, she can just pop out babies…" This is mean, not funny.

Or anytime you see someone with a drink in one hand and violently pointing a finger at someone – you're seeing some put-downs in action – someone spoiling for a fight. Angry borderlines love having fights.

This isn't loving behavior. You may be attached, but it's not love.

Rich and famous families have them

All families have some borderlines or other forms of "extreme" narcissists who are mean.

Every family is different in how they portray – and how they accept – what psychologically is "bad behavior". Your family may call someone a "jerk", when they behave meanly. Others will say that the person is "deeply flawed". Yet, some mates and families can actually say that they are spending time with genuine "haters" – which some borderlines become, as their mental illness advances.

When mental illness gets to the criminal stage, there are rich people, like the heir to the DuPont fortune who murdered a woman, or the Kennedy cousin, Michael Skakel, who murdered the girl next door who rejected his sexual advances. Both have served some prison time, despite the vast fortunes and family power at their disposal. U.S. society seems to lose its tolerance for "bad boy" or "bad girl" behavior, when the mentally ill person is very destructive.

For most people, the worst jerks in their families are often borderlines

Borderlines (1) think only of themselves, (2) love to do put-downs of others or pull something over on someone else, and (3) they totally disregard the harm they do to others. At the same time, they can be very <u>fun</u>! Corrupt (now jailed) financier Bernie Madoff, took people on fun cruises and threw lots of fantastic parties for folks, and paid big salaries.

While Bernie Madoff ripped off billions of dollars from his supposed friends, he also lied to his family – putting one over on everybody. He left his two sons in the dark, taking the blame. One of them committed suicide, because he found life so unbearable being thought to be as creepy as his father.

The wife of Prince Charles in England, Camilla Parker Bowles, is famous for impulsively drinking a lot and blurting out put-downs. She has done a lot of put-downs of her daughter-in-law.

Arnold Schwartzenegger sexually cheated, and lied and hurt all his kids.

Chaotic family get-togethers

If you have any family members with the very common borderline personality disorder, they are usually the most wild, impulsive people at any party. Yes, they will wear a lampshade. They'll put their finger in an electric socket if they are paid enough, or dared. They can be dangerous and fun!

They also often ask you to keep secrets for them about them.

This person (who may be your parent) is the one you find in a dark hallway, kissing someone's else's spouse.

They may be sipping from a liquor bottle in their purse.

They may take cash or trinkets they find at your house.

If guests leave the table for a break, they may run around and swallow the last of the wine in everybody's wine glasses.

Family exploitation

Clinging to family members, bribing or manipulating them, is how many borderlines regularly interact.

Borderlines who have any money, will use it – doling it out with heavy strings attached – to keep family members paying attention to them. Getting money from them is not a substitute for a trusting, emotional exchange between close relatives – but it is all the borderline can do. They don't trust others, so don't sincerely love, but they make attachments. Think of a puppeteer and a puppet, and you get the picture.

They detest being alone by themselves, so they try to attract family members to come around. Then they put them down, saying: "I'm just playing around – don't take it so seriously!" When they intended to score off you, so they could get a high.

They may exploit close family to put up with the mean put-downs they do to make themselves feel high, by bribes.

MORE EXPLOITATION

Since one of the traits of the borderline is impulsiveness, they usually have multiple cross addictions. They often get heart disease, have strokes, emphysema – all the diseases from addictions. They often "guilt" their kids into taking care of them since they're terrified of being alone.

Adult siblings and friends often stop talking to them.

Kids lives are not consolation prizes owed to parents.

One woman was so fed up by the time that her alcoholic mother died, that she told her still living drunk dad that if he ever got ill or fell down, to dial 911 because she wouldn't come.

The borderline's frequent bouts of bitterness push people away. You may feel their desperation, but substitute a professional to be their caretaker.

WHEN FAMILIES GET HURT BY BORDERLINES

A borderline can adore you one day, and hate you the next day – with you doing nothing at all. Describing borderlines as misbehaving and unpredictable people, may seem simple, but it's true.

At family events they'll snatch other people's drinks, pinch or grope others, smoke and flick ashes, spy in closets and into bathroom cabinets, and do LOTS of verbal put-downs. They are "creepy" guests, and every family has a couple who are close <u>relatives</u>.

Folks with borderline personality traits are so narcissistic, that they plan all their activities for what feels good to them – with zero reciprocity or concern for other people. They are known to take their dogs off-leash and literally sic them on people, for the "high".

Being around them usually makes a person feel taken for granted or victimized. Remind yourself that you don't have to see them often.

BORDERLINES CAN BE PUBLICLY HUMILIATING

A sister-in-law took photos of her husband's sister, and put one on her mantle that showed a frowning face and at an angle that looked like she had a double chin and was fat – which she wasn't. (She was a former model.) The sister-in-law went out of her way to make her relative look horrible with a terrible shot. Cruelty.

Another example was when a woman was mad at her elder sister, who she invited to drop by her apartment. The elder sister saw that the family photo on the refrigerator had been folded back, so that she was excluded from the shot. Cruelty.

Both these actions were to deliberately hurt, and be noticed by, the other person.

LESSON: don't trust a borderline.

WARNING TO CHILDREN OF BORDERLINES

Borderlines suffer depression, among other problems. Alcoholics – and 75% of borderlines are alcoholic – are also depressives. A New York Times survey found that depressed parents punished their children FOUR times more than non-depressed parents. This makes the punished kids feel bad about themselves, and in addition to low confidence they may be low in assertiveness.

Many children of borderlines have to get counseling to be able to resist the "pity-parties" and guilt-trips, done to them. One woman who had two alcoholic borderline parents, after caring for her mother till she died, told her father that she wasn't going to be like that anymore. She told him if he ever got hurt or felt bead, to just call 9-1-1. Public health services will take care of them. Kids lives are not consolation prizes owed to parents.

Two phrases that any kid from a borderline's family ought to understand:

(1) Manic-depression: depression where there are mood swings from "Mr. or Mrs. Happy!" to a person who seems to completely hate you. Sometimes this is called bi-polar disorder. The "manic" part shows when some impulsive risks are going to happen.

(2) The Glass Ceiling: this refers to when outside opportunities are denied to you and you are "kept back", which the borderline does to feel powerful.

The borderline desire to make others feel smaller so they can feel taller – their power-over others craving – makes it tough on kids. One father who was on academic probation in college for being drunk a lot, barely graduated. He told all his children that none of them needed to go to college. He didn't' want to be passed by any of them.

Some kids have Stockholm syndrome, where they feel they can only survive to adult age by underachieving in things, to not trigger anger and rage in a jealous borderline parent.

One dad co-signed on his college kid's bank account, and then emptied it. His excuse was: "I needed that money." His broke son couldn't afford his tuition for 2 semesters.

BORDERLINES CAN EXHAUST KIDS

If you grew up with a borderline in your family, the entire family was exposed to the extra emotional acting out and bad moods, that uses up everyone's energy. If your family's wage-earner was a borderline, they typically had to change jobs often – because bosses get tired of them, too.

Kids surviving these families may be tired out and not able to get easily focused on moving ahead in their own lives.

Family members or kids or even adult "friends", are seen as objects for them to verbally or physically assault – to dominate them - with groping or slapping – all for their own controlled release of tension. These households consider family members possessions, to use as they want, and their behaviors are corrosive and cruel.

KIDS COPY BORDERLINE PARENTS

Some kids copy what they saw done. One son of California borderline millionaires spent most of his income on drugs. He stole $15,000 from the pet store where he worked, to buy dope. When he was caught, his former girlfriend spent their child's college fund, to make restitution. The college fund was a gift to his child by his parents. Borderlines being toxic for two generations is not unusual. Broken love can have a ripple effect from grandparents to grandchildren; it is not trivial.

A borderline parent does have moments of being charming – and they always are willing to be intimidating – and sometimes get kids to do things for them by holding a "pity party" and saying they need to be rescued. The borderline of course recognizes that their kid is in a weaker position, and exploits it. Sometimes they become predators.

Remember that the mental illness of borderlines make them very poor at relationships. They see other people as a means to their ends. When a borderline gets very ill, they can actually get a "high" or thrills from inflicting emotional pain and even the ultimate destruction, of other people – without seeming to get their hands dirty.

Recovering from these exploitive – and sometimes life-threatening – situations, takes time. Achieving confidence again can take years. If you are the child of an alcoholic – and 75% of borderlines are alcoholic – you may not have had enough attention to feel loved, and have very low self esteem. Emotional closure and self repair doesn't happen overnight, so prepare to ask for some help and get therapy.

Kids who get straight A report cards and then get no praise from a borderline parent, can get demotivated and underachieve. The borderline parent can then make the kid "feel smaller, and make himself taller", pointing out the kid's failings, which gives the borderline a power HIGH.

STRATEGIES AND TACTICS TO CONSIDER

Gift have "strings" (conditions) attached.

In order to look "big", borderlines can sometimes give very over-the-top gifts, or may sometimes give lots of money – often to impress others.

If the borderline drinks a lot, the kid may, like one teen, get a fifth of tequila for a Christmas present.

Any family get-togethers that exchange gifts, set up potential for conflicts. On one Father's Day, the son had the gift he gave criticized, was manipulated into trimming all the shrubbery, got slapped once, and while installing software for his dad, discovered porn on his dad's PC; all within an hour.

Some families get good control over gifts by having people only exchange a single "gag" gift with the person whose name they draw. (Queen Elizabeth of England is reputed to do this at Christmas.)

The borderline, due to not trusting people much, can easily forget to ever give gifts to others, or to say thank you.

Don't get your "worth" confused with the acknowledgment you get. In love and affection the borderline adores getting attention, affection – love – but cannot reciprocate love to the same degree they receive it. That is their curse.

One borderline dad criticized every birthday gift, even a $200. silk shirt, because he enjoyed doing the put-downs, more than the presents. The daughter finally just gave him gift cards since borderlines don't refuse cash.

Another borderline said how she was going to tell everyone at the "club" about the party that her kids threw for her. She was most happy to impress her peers.

One dad was complimented by his daughter that he looked as elegant as an airline pilot. He snapped at her: "I want to look like I OWN the airline." It's about status!

One borderline went to the gym and enjoyed his workout while his sibling was slaving writing press releases for him, as a favor, and he never thanked him.

BE WARY ABOUT GIFTS AND FAVORS

One man tried to get access to his kid's credit card – to get the money – when he found the credit card receipt with the gift and called the bank. This was a man who was a millionaire. He only wanted to do it to "get one over on" his daughter. LESSON: don't trust a borderline.

Another time a rich father told his adult kids he needed to have their power of attorney, to represent them in receiving $2,000. each from property that was willed to the children. The kids trusted him. He ended up taking a slice for himself as large as their shares, for power.

Both these examples are designed to take something from the other person and shows contempt over whether they notice. LESSON: don't trust a borderline.

REMEMBER IT'S NOT YOUR FAULT

Put-downs comes from them internally; it's not aimed at anything you did. But if you happen to be physically convenient when they want to do a put-down, you may be targeted, even when they claim to love you. Slaps, pinches, and verbal put-downs are very common ways for the borderline to experience a quick, controlled release of their tension.

Telling big lies to family members is also common, to get money, or to manipulate them to make the borderline feel superior to the other person. Conning a kid out of money is also common. One millionaire father lied to his son that if he paid several thousand a month in rent on the father's beach house, that the father would sell it to him. After he "cleaned out" all the son's savings, he canceled the deal to sell him the house.

TIPS TO KEEP CALM

TIP (1): Tell yourself: "I am a human being. I am not alive to be used." Repeat this often.

TIP (2): Count quietly on your fingers during verbal put-downs, how many insults were made, and then quietly to yourself do three complimentary "put-ups" to yourself for each put-down. At the time or straight after the event.

TIP (3): Feel less bad about it. Know that professional psychologists like Dr. Martha Beck, and Dr. Phil, all agree: you do not owe spending much time or energy with people who don't treat you with respect.

TIP (4): A person can give you money or presents but still be a bad person – bad, as in mean and cruel.

TIP (5): Think of a favorite place or experience, to calm you. Repeat often that it's not your fault.

TIPS FOR YOUR PHYSICAL PROTECTION

Since you can't stop their behavior, you have to:

TIP (6): not show up at family events (claim work or illness), or say that a friend paid for you to go to an inn or someplace, and say it's non-refundable – and then DO go to someplace else.

TIP (7): show up for very brief appearances, and think to

TIP (8): bring a friend with you for reinforcement.

If you feel the need for reinforcements, that tells you that the "icky" person is a borderline. They often enjoy harming others, which is more than just being a very self centered narcissist. One hurts you, and one just bores you.

TIP (9): Hide your reaction! That frustrates them and they'll move on to another "easier" target to insult or hit.

TIPS TO PROTECT YOUR FEELINGS

TIP (10): Look at these folks as if they're just a TV show.

TIP (11): Compartmentalize – use your THINKING brain, NOT your feelings, and plan ahead.

TIP (12): One adult woman who was tired of being slapped or hit on the bottom, decided to always wear costumes – even renting them – so there was no target.

TIP (13): THINK before you speak to make NO provocative statements

TIP (14): Choose a situation where giving generously confers status upon them – and they want to look good - then ask for attention, affection, or a privilege.

TIP (15): They love big chaotic events, since those give them more freedom to misbehave, so keep things small.

BORDERLINES CAN CHANGE OVER TIME

Naturally borderlines change over time, because all people do. Researchers have found that some elderly male borderlines actually stop manipulating other people as much, and are kinder, in their 60s. You may see some changed folks in your family.

But some borderlines want ever more increasing power over others by putting others down, and do not become kinder. They get "worse", making others feel smaller so they can feel taller. This group may include less powerful older people. Some people get more bitter and grasping for power and attention, as they get older.

At family holidays, you can see where older family members get away with actions that younger people are not allowed. (Pretend it's all just a poor quality TV show. As Shakespeare said: "If you feel, life's a tragedy, but if you THINK - life's a comedy.")

BIBLIOGRAPHY

Ann Ford, in her book "**If a Borderline Loves You**", deals with family and love relationships with borderlines and other difficult people.

Dr. Charles Whitfield specializes in helping victims of childhood trauma. His books include "***Healing the Child Within***", "***Memory and Abuse***", and "***The Truth About Mental Illness***".

The ***Diagnostic and Statistical Manual of Mental Disorders*** (DSM) specifies diagnostic and statistical data for doctors.

Olivier Ameisen claimed in his book ***The Last Glass*** that he had cured himself of alcoholism by treating himself with high doses of the drug baclofen.

Psychology Today is a general interest magazine that covers the range of human behavior.

Dr. Robert O. Friedel is the author of the book ***Borderline Personality Disorder Demystified***. He is a psychiatrist specializing in effective pharmacological treatments.

Tina Fey wrote in her book ***Bossypants*** about working with brutal people.

AUTHOR'S BIO

Ann Ford

Ford has a M.S. in counseling psychology, Phi Kappa Phi, and did post-graduate work and instructed at Johns Hopkins in adult learning styles. She has counseled over 300 clients, primarily as part of large business downsizings, helping people through grief, forced change, and how to start over. She has lectured to university psychology departments on the cycle of domestic violence, taught court-ordered DV offenders new skills and taught the domestic violence cycle to incoming police recruits, and has conducted seminars nationally on sexual harassment.

She's been published in many publications, has been a columnist, and in recent years has won a few literary awards, writing books on multiple subjects, including a children's book on Hiroshima.

She's been nominated for a broadcasting award from American Women in Radio and Television, and won a Communications Arts Award, for work in her first career, which was radio and television broadcasting.

Made in the USA
San Bernardino, CA
17 October 2014